Narcissism

Understanding Narcissism And Permanently Escaping The Narcissist In A Toxic Relationship: A Comprehensive Survival Guide

Rickey Oconnor

TABLE OF CONTENT

When It Is Time To Depart 10

The Narcissist 24

The Report's Development Phase And Whether Or Not It Is Rational To Correct It 56

Take Control Back 71

Self-Soothing Work With Your Inner Child 77

The Effects Of Having Narcissistic Parents As A Child 102

What Self-Centered Mothers Do 120

Chapter 5: Making Amends 127

Developing Stable Relationships 136

What Effect Does Narcissism Have On Your Relationship? 162

Implications Of Living With A Narcissist 174

Not long after Nationals, Melanie admitted she had begun listening to Rock. At this time, he was assisting her with housework. Rock had little mechanical aptitude. He was more like a bull in a china shop, but Melanie needed assistance while I was away. They owned

"only recently began seeing each other. Everyone was aware by this point that Rock began his courtship on the treadmills of the gym.

Over the past few months, I've learned from a variety of sources that Melanie has been discussing our marital issues with anyone who would listen. There are always three sides to every narrative, and while I kept our disagreements to myself, she did not.

When Rock learned that this successful career woman was experiencing problems, she became an ideal target.

Rock was a man who knew everything and could solve any issue. He was well-organized, punctual, tidy, and productive. He was my opposite.

The day was Saturday. The children were viewing television in the family room when Melanie and Rock entered the home. My children gazed up as Melanie requested their attention. Melanie waited for the children to glance up before introducing Tess and Sam to her friend Rock. This is Tess and Sam, rocking it. They exchanged pleasantries, after which Melanie and Rock walked into the kitchen while the children exchanged awkward glances. Melanie ascended the stairs, and Rock returned to the Great Room. The children viewing television detected the presence of a person in the great room. Rock approached the television, and the children peered up. He looked at them and said, "Hey, guys, I'm going to be helping your mother a lot more. If there is anything you folks require, I will provide assistance.

I just wanted to inform you that there will soon be a new man around here. Afterward, he exited the room.

Tess and Sam exchanged glances and giggles. Tess regarded Sam and remarked, "He has no idea."

As soon as Rock met the family, word spread. Melanie was involved with another individual. She would only discuss how flawless he was. How she never did any work. He would clean up following supper.

He began transporting her to and from the train station each morning and evening. Melanie was welcomed off the train each evening with freshly cut bouquets. He became a household fixture. Rock was rearranging the furniture, cleaning the veranda, and washing the automobiles. He thoroughly enjoyed washing the vehicles. He was flawless in every way, and Melanie began to brag about her new boyfriend. She began to introduce him to our old crowd, the crowd that believed I was terrible and this man was Mr. Perfect.

Melanie would receive daily compliments regarding Rock's attractiveness. Everyone except Rob enjoyed Rock. Rob was a Neighborhood acquaintance and our landscaper. Rob was a throwback. You must have earned his respect. He was the only person who did not abandon me in the end. Together, we would share anecdotes about how Rock was untrustworthy.

One evening, Rob and his wife invited Melanie and Rock over for a barbecue and beverages. Melanie strolled in gleaming. They were greeted at the door by Rob's wife. Rock was introduced to Rob's fiancée by Melanie. After a brief discussion, everyone enters the backyard where Rob was beginning to fire up the grill. Rob and Melanie were close companions. They were admirers of Dave Mathews, and we all visited Jones Beach annually. They ate while making small conversation. Melanie hung around Rock the entire night. Melanie was told by the wife of Robs, "You look so happy." She responded, "Yes, he is perfect." It's as if he fulfills every requirement I've ever had for a companion. It's as if he fell from the heavens. The evening concluded, and Melanie and Rock departed. Rob's wife turned to him as the door closed and said, "She looks so happy."

Rob gazed in disbelief. He replied, "I don't get it. I just don't get it?"

Who is this person? He spoke very little tonight. He merely sat there and attended to her every need. I dislike this individual. I just don't get it.

A week later, it was time to expand the friend group introductions. The Franks were hosting a barbecue for several couples. Obviously, I was not invited, but Melanie and Rock were. Again, Rock was paraded among the visitors, and again he waited on Melanie hand and foot. Melanie, who enjoyed wine, was consuming significantly less than usual. Melanie was intent on displaying her new beau. Rock was preoccupied with Melanie and hardly interacted with anyone else at the barbecue.

His top priority was Melanie and ensuring he could provide her with anything she desired.

Everyone at the barbecue told Melanie how joyful she appeared, but all she could say was that he was great. It was the realization of a fantasy. All he wishes to do is serve as my waiter. His beauty is me.

My children had spent the weekend with me. I was looking forward to spending time with them. When they arrived at my parents' residence, they were all smiles.

I inquired as to why the children were in such a pleasant mood. The children informed me that Rock had purchased new televisions for each of their rooms, and this was only the beginning. The only thing I heard all weekend was how fantastic Rock is and how they will be releasing new music. It was becoming increasingly revolting. Who the hell is this person?

When It Is Time To Depart

Relationship termination is always difficult. Even if your spouse's NPD has caused you significant harm, you may still have a great deal of affection for them, but when their behavior crosses the line into mental or physical abuse, it is time to leave.

Occasionally, you must determine whether or not the connection is likely to strengthen. When someone acts aggressively or threatens violence, it's time to flee.

Some red flags to watch for in the other party include:

feeling isolated from family and acquaintances

Questioning your self-worth having difficulty enjoying activities feeling afraid to be yourself or act a certain way around your partner frequently feeling guilty for expressing your opinion or needs monitoring your movements or attempting to isolate you telling you how you feel or should feel routinely projecting their shortcomings onto you denying things that are obvious or attempting to gaslight you

Generally, it is preferable to terminate a relationship if:

You are experiencing verbal or emotional maltreatment.

You feel controlled and manipulated.

You have been abused physically or feel threatened.

The individual with NPD or a narcissistic personality demonstrates symptoms of mental illness or substance misuse, but refuses assistance.

Your physical or mental health has been compromised.

Chapter 12 Work Environment W

Bullying by narcissists in the workplace is distressingly common if you have worked for a large multinational corporation. The issue with workplace abuse is that it is not as simple to simply disconnect the bully. Finding a new work at the drop of a hat is impractical for a large number of individuals who rely on their incomes.

This is notably true during economic downturns. In such circumstances, narcissists are frequently emboldened, and you will be pushed into a corner. I'm going to discuss the causes of workplace bullying as well as plausible solutions to this problem.

Confronting Abuse

Some HR departments are equipped to manage incidents of workplace bullying, but narcissism in the workplace is typically covert and passive-aggressive and cannot always be openly labeled as bullying. Given the nature of the abuse, victims frequently query whether or not it is appropriate to report it, particularly if they are male.

The initial interactions follow the same pattern of narcissistic abuse in which the love bomb is used to entice the victim. While there are no flowers or presents involved, the narcissist will attempt to endear themselves to the victim by eliciting an abundance of information about themselves.

Typically, the finest and most productive employees are targeted, so if you are highly qualified for the position, you must be vigilant. Once the narcissist has acquired sufficient information about their victim and has developed a close relationship with them, rumors will begin to circulate, and you will be undermined by them.

This may occur initially in a meeting where the abuser claims credit for your work or undermines you subtly in front of your superiors. In such situations, when you stand up to them, rumors will circulate and people will speak about you behind your back.

This is exceedingly difficult if your abuser is also your boss. While a supervisor will be threatened by your competence, their superior authority will reassure them somewhat regarding the security of their position, so you may not hear as many rumors. After all, few individuals socialize with their supervisor outside of the workplace.

A key indicator is the classic narcissistic tendency to alternate between adoring and hating you. If you disappoint them in any way, the floodgates will open and the criticism will be extremely personal. Selfishness is yet another red flag. If the subject of every conversation is how wonderful they are or how much superior they are than you, you are almost certainly dealing with a potential abuser.

Many companies require evaluation forms, and some even have forms that demand feedback about your supervisor. This is an ideal time to identify the narcissist. They will be unable to tolerate any criticism and will be extremely offended by it. When it comes to coworkers, look for indications of someone who craves leadership and will tolerate nothing less.

Such individuals might or might not be certified, but qualification is secondary. The most important factor is their ability to rule over everyone else. Unfortunately, modern workplaces reward this type of behavior because it is regarded as a form of ambition and positive energy that must be channeled for the benefit of the company. Unfortunately, all it does is make everyone's lives a living misery.

It is essential to observe that not all narcissists are bullies. Many covert narcissists will be satisfied with undermining their coworkers and advancing at all costs. A skilled narcissist is unlikely to engage in this type of verbal harassment because, in the majority of workplaces today, calling someone a derogatory name is grounds for instantaneous dismissal.

Frequently, such individuals are placed in positions for which they are grossly unqualified, causing the inevitable chaos. A narcissist's inability to express remorse or take responsibility for their actions is a glaring red flag.

Confronting Workplace Narcissism

The easiest method to deal with a narcissist at work is to avoid them whenever possible. This is not always practicable, particularly if the individual involved is your boss. Dealing with such a situation is extremely difficult, and unless you cannot imagine leaving your job, the best course of action is to find something else as quickly as possible. In the end, you will not have the same amount of energy as the narcissist, and you will be the one who is fatigued from all the maneuvering.

When dealing with a narcissist in the workplace, well-meaning acquaintances may advise you not to allow yourself to be spoken to in such a manner, etc., but this will only make matters worse. Instead, attempt to refocus the narcissist as much as possible on the task at hand. This is especially for instances in which their criticism becomes personal. You will accomplish nothing by yelling back or demanding an apology from them. So, do not anticipate it.

Instead, encourage them to concentrate on the current task and avoid them as much as possible. In the case of colleagues, document every piece of work you complete, every action you take, and every suggestion you make. This will help you maintain your composure when confronting the colleague and telling them to stop stealing your ideas. If you fail to do so, they may cause you to become confused and doubt your own beliefs.

If your coworker is the source of the problem, you should approach your supervisors with your suggestions before approaching the coworker. If a coworker asks you about your ideas, be brief or even deflect the query. However, never convey the impression that you are prepared to fight them. Remember that every feeling is fuel for them. Your best defense is to engage as little as possible and to be as apathetic as possible when you do.

Sadly, given the narcissists' ability to manipulate and disguise their desire for power as ambition, your superiors will frequently fell for it and promote them. If you observe such promotions occurring frequently, you must accept that you will not be treated fairly at your current place of employment. In such situations, it is recommended to find an alternative as soon as possible.

Obviously, in many situations, your supervisor is a narcissist. If the failure of a work-related endeavor is due to your supervisor's incompetence, direct criticism will accomplish nothing. If anything, it will place you in their sights, and your life will become increasingly miserable. When presenting new ideas, do not imply that the previous idea was bad or ineffective.

Even better would be to cast doubt on your own idea and then leave it up to them to decide, as if you were seeking their counsel. This will increase your likelihood of being viewed favorably and having things accomplished.

Ultimately, this tap dancing is absurd, and you owe it to yourself to find a more suitable place of employment. Remember that being kind to yourself entails placing yourself in an environment that allows your talents to shine, and that a workplace filled with insecure bullies is not such an environment.

Given the prevalence of narcissism in the workplace, if you're new to a position, you should be cautious about revealing personal information to colleagues or superiors. In the long run, assuming the workplace is a good fit for you, you will be more than able to make restitution for any initial aloofness.

Family abuse and workplace abuse are difficult situations, but there is no situation more sticky than being in an abusive romantic relationship. Given the immense quantity of emotion we invest in our relationships, they are the most difficult to escape.

The Narcissist

Some individuals crave attention more than others. Admiration, feeling significant, and feeling unique. Wouldn't it be incredible if someone made you his universe's focal point? All of these are feelings and emotions that individuals experience from time to time. Normal is the desire to feel special. Everyone experiences it at some stage. You may even go out of your way to do things that make you feel incredible.

What occurs when things become out of control? The desire to feel unique manifests as manipulation, arrogance, and a desire to have everything go your way. At this juncture, it is no longer about being the center of attention; it could be a mental illness. There is a possibility that you suffer from narcissistic personality disorder (NPD).

NPD is a significant disorder. Because it only affects about 1% of the world's population, it is rarely discussed (Wright & Furnham, 2015). Individuals with NPD have an inflated desire to experience all the aforementioned positive emotions, typically at the expense of others. Everything about the individual is exaggerated as a result of the lack of empathy. For such individuals, vanity, prestige, power, and fame are among the most important things in the universe.

As with the majority of mental disorders, NPD can be puzzling because the symptoms may also be observed in individuals with genuine self-confidence or high self-esteem. Possibly one of the differences between these individuals and those with NPD is that despite having sky-high confidence and self-esteem, they remain modest. On the other hand, individuals with NPD are egotistical, self-centered, and will do anything to gain attention. Their demands must always take precedence.

On the surface, it may appear that a person exhibiting the definitive symptoms of NPD is overconfident and has a strong belief in their own abilities (Wright & Fursham, 2015). This is, however, merely a smokescreen for profoundly rooted insecurity. Their insecurities are especially apparent when they are provoked or in a situation where it appears that they will not prevail. This is when they employ their manipulative abilities in an attempt to influence the situation in their favor.

In general, if you have NPD, it will negatively impact your existence. (Schroeter & Thomson, 2018) You feel a surge of discontent when you need others to recognize your efforts but they don't. You can use temper outbursts to garner attention for mundane matters. The elevated sense of self-importance produces a persona that the majority of individuals cannot tolerate. Before you know it, your surroundings suffer. From your work to your personal and professional relationships, people avoid interacting with you.

It is difficult for those with NPD because the disorder obscures their ability to recognize their role in the circumstances that drive people away. The detrimental effects of NPD affect not only the people you interact with, but also you. When people cannot abide you and consistently find reasons to avoid you, you feel unfulfilled, emptied out, and in some cases, worthless.

causes and classification

Although experts believe that environmental and genetic factors may play a role in NPD, no definitive cause has been identified. Genetics and the environment in which people with NPD operate provide an abundance of potential causes, making it impossible to pinpoint the exact cause.

The onset of NPD symptoms that persist into adulthood occurs during the developmental stages of life, and by the time the individual reaches maturity, the traits are completely embraced. Conflict in interpersonal development may also be to blame for these characteristics, given that the individual struggles to make sense of certain actions, emotions, reactions, and responses to them in life (Linden, 2010). The following are examples of destructive conflicts that may occur in life and lead to NPD:

- A child acclimated to receiving excessive compliments on their abilities or appearance.

- Lack of a genuine feedback system to combat excessive admiration.

- Overindulgence by family and peers, resulting in an inflated sense of self-importance.

- Unpredictable, inconsistent, and unreliable parental or guardian care.

- Having endured childhood abuse.

- Living between extremes of praise and criticism for positive and bad actions.

- Learning to manipulate others through imitation of peers and parents.

- Children born with a temperament that is extremely sensitive.

According to experts, people with NPD do not have the same quantity of gray matter in their left anterior insula as healthy individuals. According to Miller and Maples (2012), the left anterior insula is responsible for modulating compassion, emotions, empathy, and cognitive abilities. With this deficiency, it is understandable that patients with NPD will struggle to express or recognize these emotions, even when they are the only ones conceivable.

In terms of prevalence rates, more males than women suffer from NPD. NPD affects younger individuals more than elderly ones. People with NPD typically do not realize they have a problem. Although therapy is recommended, it is extremely difficult for them to seek assistance. However, it is essential to distinguish between NPD and narcissistic personality type.

NPD is about extremes. Enhancing the definitive characteristics. Excessive reliance on the accolades of others. Feeling exceptional and superior, maintaining superficial relationships, and displaying little or no empathy. NPD represents the most extreme form of narcissism. It results in functional impairment and distress, and its effects are very long-lasting.

Personality traits of narcissistic individuals

Are you in a personal or professional relationship with someone who believes they are superior to others and demands constant admiration and attention? Do you believe the person is constantly condescending, belittling others if things are not done their way, and throwing tantrums at the slightest sign of criticism or disagreement? There are strong indications that you may be dealing with a narcissist.

There are distinct characteristics that can be used to identify individuals with NPD. Typically, these individuals indulge in a perverted form of power play to get their way. As their victim, you must learn to recognize these personalities from a distance and establish healthy boundaries in order to coexist peacefully.

Remember that individuals with NPD are more likely to resist change (Yang and Kwon, 2016). They are content with their behavior, and they believe that you, who are requesting that they be accommodating, may have a problem. You may believe it is acceptable to comply with a narcissist's demands in order to avoid their anger, coldness, and tantrums, but this is an unhealthy coping mechanism. In actuality, you only make matters worse by doing so, as they will then realize that they have power over you.

Listed below are some signs that a narcissist may be present in your immediate environment:

- Self-importance

In addition to being arrogant and egotistical, narcissists have an unrealistic view of themselves. They believe they are superior to everyone and everything. They believe that they are unique and can only be comprehended by other unique individuals, who are also the only individuals worthy of interacting with them.

Narcissists enjoy associating with high-status objects, locations, and individuals. They have no time for everyday activities. Since they believe they are superior to everyone else, they believe it is only appropriate that they receive the regal treatment, even though they have not done much to merit it.

To satiate their ego, narcissists will exaggerate their personal achievements when discussing them (Bardi, 2015). Their description includes how fortunate people are to have them in their lives, as well as their contributions and greatness.

• Delusions of majesty

Reality will never match narcissists' grandiose perception of themselves. Considering this, they flourish on fantasy. Their universe is permeated by self-deception, enchantment, distortion, and illusions. Everything about their existence is a fantasy, with one concept remaining constant: their power, brilliance, limitless success, and beauty. They have everything.

The significance of such fantasies is that they shield the narcissist from confronting their reality, which is a life devoid of meaning and filled with remorse and shame. Anything factual that contradicts their conception of who they are must be either rationalized away or ignored. The same disdain is applied to objects or individuals that threaten to burst their fantasy world. This explains why individuals who interact with narcissists are constantly on edge.

- Prerogative and superiority

Narcissists have a predetermined hierarchy for all aspects of their existence. Their existence consist of extremes. It is either better or worse, superior or inferior. The narcissist is at the summit of this hierarchy, wielding as much power as an overlord. They can only feel secure at the highest point.

They must be correct, the most capable, the finest, and in charge of everything. Narcissists derive the same pleasure from being the absolute worst at everything. They believe they have the right to cause you harm and demand an apology from you in order to make things even.

• Individualism over group effort

A team concept necessitates harmonious coexistence between team members. Conflicts may arise from time to time, as they are normal and healthy in an environment where people join together to exchange ideas. Understanding what other team members feel, why they feel that way, and respecting their decisions are of greater importance.

Teamwork requires compromise as well. Occasionally, for the greater good, you must allow another person to triumph at your expense. However, narcissists lack the ability to recognize delayed gratification. A narcissist is not concerned with questions such as whether a given action will make everyone pleased. No one else matters to them.

Narcissists are incapable of considering or being motivated by the greater good. They are only concerned with their victories. They cannot surrender a position, especially a strong or victorious position, in order for someone else to prevail. This is why such individuals find it simpler to thrive independently than in groups.

- characteristics of perfectionists

Narcissists will go to extraordinary extent to ensure that everything is flawless. Their perception of themselves is flawless. Everyone else ought to be flawless. All surrounding festivities must proceed as planned. Life must unfold according to their plan.

Perfection is an impossible goal to reach. Since no one is flawless, narcissists will be perpetually miserable and dissatisfied with life. This is why they always have something or someone to complain about. In the existence of a narcissist, dissatisfaction is the norm.

- Obsessive control freaks

Life is not flawless. This means a narcissist will experience constant disappointment. The solution is to maintain control. Narcissists attempt to exert control over their surroundings. Similar to puppet controllers. Their plan must be followed to the letter. The only thing that works for them is what is logical.

There is a protocol that must be followed when interacting with a narcissist. It unnerves them when you deviate from the script, because it disturbs them. They want to be in charge, but you throw them curveballs, so they have no idea what to expect from you. In their imaginations, narcissists have an ideal conclusion. To accomplish this, everyone must act and speak in accordance with their moral beliefs.

In your interactions with a narcissist, you are not a thinking and feeling individual. You perform a role in their play. You act and speak as instructed. You believe as is expected of you.

• Deflection and attribution

Narcissists are rife with inner turmoil. On the one hand, they have a strong desire to maintain authority. On the other hand, they must not be held accountable for results, particularly if things do not go as planned. If everything works out, then they must be recognized for their hard labor.

Situations in which things do not go as planned are unpleasant for narcissists. Because of this, there is always someone else to blame. Occasionally, they assign blame to a broad spectrum, such as all instructors, all supervisors, or all children. In some instances, they assign responsibility to a specific individual.

The most prolific victim in a narcissist's life is the person they are emotionally dearest to. Typically, this is the most loving and loyal individual in their existence. It is simpler for them to blame you for their flaws because they know you love them too much to ever leave or reject them. In doing so, the appearance of their perfection enjoys another day in the sun.

• Lack of regard for boundaries

Where do their limits end and yours begin? Concerning boundaries, there is no distinction between a narcissist and a two-year-old going through the phase of "monkey see, monkey do." Everyone shares their sentiments, desires the same things, and everything is theirs. Woe to you if you hold an opposing viewpoint.

No comes as a shock to a narcissist, and they are profoundly insulted by it. Narcissists will do whatever it takes to get what they want, including sulking, rejection, demanding, persistence, and cajoling.

• Invulnerability

To adore someone, you must emotionally connect with them. When you share an emotional connection with someone, you open your existence to them. You expose your vulnerability. You expose your weaknesses in order for them to comprehend and appreciate you for who you are, faults and all. This is a level of comprehension that narcissists do not possess.

Narcissists cannot comprehend emotions. Their need for self-preservation outweighs their capacity for empathy (Miller & Maples, 2012). Expecting them to see the world from your perspective is futile. Emotionally, narcissists lack empathy. They are alone in a world where no one recognizes their uniqueness, which they cannot comprehend. In consequence, narcissists are emotionally demanding but incapable of being vulnerable.

If a narcissist believes their current relationship does not fulfill their needs, it is simple for them to walk away or seek gratification by forming a new relationship and merging the two. Someone must experience their pain, demonstrate empathy, and rectify the situation in order to make them comfortable. However, do not expect them to repay your kindness.

- Lack of compassion

Narcissists are so preoccupied with their own lives that they cannot empathize with others. A narcissist is incapable of feeling or recognizing what you feel. When interacting with a narcissist, you are expected to mirror their actions and emotions.

For those lacking empathy, narcissists have a heightened awareness of others' wrath, rejection, and perceived threats. They are nearly oblivious to the emotions of those around them, misinterpreting simple gestures and facial expressions as negative bias towards them. The only way a narcissist can recognize your emotions is if you act them out dramatically.

Saying I love you or I'm sorry could easily backfire if a narcissist is on the verge of a mental collapse. They believe that your feelings are insincere and that you are concealing an attack.

Additionally, narcissists expect your expressions and words to coincide. Without this, they always provide an incorrect response. This explains why the majority of narcissists interpret sarcasm as truth and humor as personal attacks.

In addition to their incapacity to comprehend your emotions, narcissists cannot comprehend their own emotions or how they develop. In the perception of a narcissist, their emotions are the result of the actions of something or someone else. Narcissists cannot accept the fact that emotions are a culmination of interpretations, thoughts, and complex biochemistry.

Someone else is always accountable for their emotions, particularly their negative emotions. You are responsible for their vulnerability because you did not execute their plan. Consequently, you are to fault. Therefore, establishing a deep rapport with a narcissist is impossible. Simply stated, they are indifferent to your emotions.

- Emotional incapacitation

Reason and logic are irrelevant to a narcissist. This is why many attempts to convey to narcissists how their behavior affects others fail. Most people, especially empaths, make the error of believing that if the narcissist understands how you feel, they will alter their behavior and be considerate.

This makes no logic to the narcissist. The only things they are cognizant of are their desires, emotions, and thoughts. A narcissist may occasionally respond to your argument with a subtle I understand. However, they do not in their hearts.

The majority of decisions made by narcissists are based on how they feel about something or someone. Suppose they wish to purchase a home in a prosperous neighborhood, for instance. To them, they must own that property because it makes them feel good, and they also enjoy living in a wealthy neighborhood. This decision is based on how they feel, regardless of whether the purchase is financially prudent for the family or their budget (He & Zhu, 2016).

If a narcissist is depressed, bored, wants to start a new business, or wants to end a relationship, they will turn outside of themselves to satisfy this need. Their expectations are expressed as demands. If you are with them, they expect you to embrace their decision as the optimal course of action. Expect surges of aggressive resentment and irritation if you do not.

- Split personalities

Everything in a narcissist's existence is either good or bad. This is a result of their inherent disposition. From here, they classify everything else, particularly relationships, as either positive or negative. A narcissist will always claim credit for anything good or positive, but will always find someone to blame for their own negative thoughts, actions, and behavior. In response to your disapproval, they deny all of the negative actions and words they portray and instead refute it. If they do something improper, it is your responsibility. You are not a decent person because you cannot see the good in others and are constantly searching for reasons to blame them for something.

In a narcissist's psyche, the concept of good and evil cannot coexist. It is either terrible, amazing, or excellent. Even when presented with both positive and negative outcomes, narcissists are incapable of recognizing this. Only one perspective matters in their lives – their own!

Self-Awareness

You can develop immunity to narcissists in the same way that your body has an immune system to help it fight off various infections and diseases. When properly maintained, such as by consuming nutritious foods, imbibing enough water, and getting sufficient rest, the body can actively support the immune system, allowing it to generate potent defenses. You can similarly safeguard your mental health from the narcissist's poisonous influence.

The modern world has an expanding presence of toxins. There are narcissists everywhere, and although they do not have NPD, their selfishness can still affect you. Obviously, you are not required to be in their presence. You can sometimes choose to avoid their negativity. In contrast to those who can easily break up with or sever ties with their narcissist fiancé or roommate, you cannot do the same with narcissist parents, siblings, spouses, or coworkers.

You cannot avoid being in their presence, but you can undoubtedly develop resistance. The inquiry is "how?" Permit me to direct your actions.

Recognizing and Appreciating Your Identity

Developing psychological and mental resistance to narcissists and other noxious individuals begins with you. It is essential to comprehend and value one's true identity. Your essence is not your life's accomplishments, but your demeanor and character. Who you are is comprised of your integrity and fortitude, your kindness and compassion, and your capacity to look the truth in the face.

Everyone is capable of becoming as ruthless and vicious as a narcissist. We desire membership in an exclusive group, to be admired and cherished. Realize that this is true for everyone, but do not neglect to remind yourself to never sacrifice your identity for this. The appreciation of others may make you temporarily joyful, but it cannot fill your heart. You will have the first line of defense against the toxicity of others only when you know and accept what you can and cannot do.

Concentrate on Becoming a Robust, Strong Person

The next step is to become a person with a strong, unshakeable conviction in yourself. Your objective is to become a mentally and emotionally robust individual, resistant to the negativity in your environment. Developing resilience will require you to concentrate on developing a variety of skills.

It involves developing self-confidence and learning to view yourself favorably. In addition, it is essential to learn how to communicate and control your impulses and emotions. Developing mental fortitude is a side effect of learning to solve problems effectively.

Only your reaction is completely under your control in life. When you learn how to effectively manage your emotions, nothing in the world can depress you.

Not the self-centeredness of a narcissist whose aim is to get you to react and focus on them.

When you have greater emotional control, it is simple to disregard their taunts regardless of what they do. While it is commendable that you are attempting to improve your perceived shortcomings, you should also take the time to recognize your strengths. Review all of your strengths and congratulate yourself on them.

When appropriate, clap yourself on the back or reward yourself for your accomplishments. Learning to accept your limitations and celebrate your strengths enables you to have complete mental and emotional control.

Establish an impregnable inner space

Consider your mind or psyche to be a home, with each room representing your impenetrable inner space. No one can ever harm you there. When the narcissist attacks, having a secure haven is useful. Create inner space by establishing routines and behaviors that can calm the mind. This is illustrated by meditation.

Regarding the body, regular exercise can be of tremendous benefit. Similarly, eating nutritious foods and having sufficient rest can strengthen the mind, body, and mind. When you have a healthy body and mind, you will have a healthy psyche that can withstand any storm. Self-empowerment and inspiration can also be achieved through creative pursuits such as painting.

When you have other things to concentrate on besides the words and actions of a narcissist, they are unable to deceive or manipulate you. When the environment is dreadful, seek out the light within yourself. A listening ear is another method to calm your mind against the cruelty of a narcissist when you cannot find it within yourself.

Keep your mind open to your own creativity and imagination. When you do so, the results will be unexpected.

The Report's Development Phase And Whether Or Not It Is Rational To Correct It

Clearly, there is no assurance that you will not fall for a two-faced individual again if you encounter one. Despite our level of education, exposure, knowledge, personal experience, and age, we cannot help but develop a romantic relationship. When a person demonstrates early love and affection, it is normal to develop feelings of attraction or attachment.

A narcissist does not have any special abilities that they use to manipulate us and transform us into puppets without free will. Typically, the narcissist is aware of how we feel and how eager we are to please.

The narcissist simply arouses your emotions by lavishing you with praise and making you feel cherished. In order to form a connection with another person, we must be emotionally available and receptive, which exposes us to the possibility of sorrow. However, this does not necessarily imply that you will experience emotional trauma.

Relationships involve heartbreak, but psychological trauma is an entirely different situation. The feelings of sorrow, disappointment, and pain associated with heartbreak when a relationship ends do not necessitate psychological destruction.

Not all narcissists' abusive behavior is scandalous and insensitive. Some present a subdued, peaceful, and innocent appearance when surrounded by strangers. In fact, this is how the majority of people fell into the narcissist's trap.

You chose to console them and view them as victims, despite the fact that they are to blame for what transpired, instead of noticing all the handwriting on the wall staring at you. As a narcissist, he or she is incapable of altering his or her negative behaviors.

Nothing will alter because you are dealing with a narcissist and not a typical person.

The manner in which narcissists experience emotion differs significantly from that of average individuals, and this is reflected in their behavior. In light of this, you should not respond to a narcissist in the same way you respond to other individuals and expect the same results.

Map Guide For Survivors To Recover Their Dreams And Decisions And Reconstruct Their Lives

Have you previously been victimized by a narcissist and do not wish for that to happen again? Using the below recommendations, we can avoid narcissists and remain off their radar.

Resist the temptation to take care of someone you've just met:

If you are in a relationship with someone and he or she tells you about the difficulties they are facing at work, school, or with their health, and that they need extra care from you, you should ask yourself why you should be the one to fulfill these roles and why no one was doing so before you entered their life.

This is a common method employed by narcissists to get near to others. When you hear the following statements, it is a warning sign and you should be more cautious:

I recently lost my employment and require a loan.

I recently relocated to the area and need a place to remain.

My previous partner and I had a joint account, but they fled with everything.

My previous partner was so dreadful that I lost interest in romantic relationships.

When you hear something related to the previous statement, insist that you are not a rebound individual and flee as quickly as possible.

Do not reveal your private information prematurely:

If you have information that you can't share with your school or workplace colleagues, you shouldn't share it with your new partner within the first couple of weeks.

When you reveal confidential information, there are typically two outcomes. First, sharing personal information creates a sense of intimacy and is the quickest method to become close to someone. A narcissist always employs this technique to quickly bond with their victims. It is never a good idea to get too close to someone you barely know. It never ends well. The second effect is that the shared private information can be used against you, particularly if the recipient is a narcissist. You will eventually regret revealing your personal information in this manner.

A narcissist has a propensity to reveal information that you consider to be extremely private, causing you to feel compelled to disclose similar information.

A successful relationship is based on intimacy and trust, but to err on the side of caution, take your time, as there will be ample opportunity in the future to reveal all the information you desire.

Maintain your private space:

Moving in with someone you just met or agreeing to have that person move in with you within a brief period of time after the meeting, resulting in the person making the move seem permanent, is a warning sign. inform the individual to make other plans or inform him or her directly that it is too early to take such a step.

When you allow a narcissist to move in with you, you give them the power to control your existence. You will eventually realize that they have taken over and are now living with you full-time, making it difficult to maintain your own space. The longer they remain at your location, the more challenging it is for you to maintain your position.

Having someone move in with you shortly after meeting does not demonstrate commitment; rather, it does not give you enough time to reconcile the relationship with other aspects of your life.

Appreciate reciprocity:

When beginning a new relationship, allow for mutuality. When he or she compliments you, you respond with a compliment of your own. When they perform a service for you, you can return the favor. You can check up on them when they check up on you.

Survivor

Normally, everyone desires a healthy relationship, but when the relationship is new, it is prudent to maintain equilibrium. When you treat them similarly to how they treat you, you will be in the loop and able to determine whether the sensation is positive.

Consider, for example, when they lavish you with so many gifts that you observe or feel uneasy about it; this is a red flag. Thus, you are able to move beyond the joy you experience when receiving gifts and take the situation into careful consideration.

Taking a step back may be necessary if you observe that you are the one who always gives gifts and you do not experience any sense of reciprocity.

Also, if you feel that you are giving too many compliments and not receiving any in return, this may be anomalous and a warning sign.

It is very easy to get sucked into the vortex of a new relationship, and you may abruptly realize that everything about you has changed. To avoid falling for a narcissist, it is crucial to arm yourself with knowledge at the outset.

Do not strive for the relationship at the outset.

This could be a sign if the person you are in a relationship with expresses concern that you will break up with them or that their family or acquaintances disapprove of your union. This is a common tactic employed by narcissists to force their partners to work harder for the relationship. They want to hear early on that you will always be there for them no matter what, or that you will give them that assurance.

Why would you choose a partner whose family and acquaintances disapprove of you? Why would you wish to be surrounded by individuals who detest you and make you feel like an outcast? In the early stages of a relationship, if the other person is already sounding fearful and asking for assurances, it is too soon to make such a commitment, and you should refrain from doing so. Giving promises will make you feel bound and make it difficult to break your word, even if you so desire.

If you feel pressured to make an early commitment with someone you are unsure of, you should always stand your ground and view this as a warning sign.

Continue your current activities:

When you notice that your new partner wants to see you or speak to you every minute, this is a sign of pathology, not admiration or love. At the outset of a relationship, it is excessive to spend nearly all of your time with the other person.

Narcissists will always want you all to themselves and tend to exert complete control over their partner's actions. Their ultimate aim is to eliminate everyone else from your life so that you become completely dependent on them.

In a healthy relationship, your partner will want you to maintain friendships, have an existence outside of the relationship, and pursue your interests.

The aforementioned information on how to avoid falling for a narcissist again will assist you in avoiding a relationship with a narcissist and avoiding their attention. Keep in mind that not all relationships are beneficial; some will cause you more harm than good. Always make a U-turn when directed to do so.

Key Point

It is essential to maintain vigilance against narcissists.

Implementation Steps

Be occasionally lenient with the narcissist, even when they are at fault.

Define your limitations.

Take Control Back

Emotional abuse is extremely detrimental, and if you do not undergo the healing process, you become even more susceptible to entering a similar relationship. You will experience anxiety, depression, dissociation, feelings of low self-esteem, low self-worth, nightmares, and flashbacks due to psychological abuse. You must seek counseling to aid in the healing process; however, there are daily strategies you can implement to help you progress forward.

Yoga

Yoga is a combination of physical activity and mindfulness that helps to restore homeostasis in the body after trauma. Yoga reduces anxiety and depression, improves symptoms of post-traumatic stress disorder in victims of domestic violence, increases self-esteem, and enhances body image, according to research. Yoga entails a series of forceful movements that compensate for the powerlessness that abuse victims experience.

Dr. Bessel Van der Kolk has spent years researching the benefits of yoga, and he believes that it enables victims of trauma to regain control of their bodies. Through the use of bodily sensations, yoga helps abuse victims regain a sense of protection, which trauma robs them of.

The region of the brain responsible for memory, learning, emotion regulation, and planning is disrupted by trauma. The same regions of the brain that are affected by trauma, such as the hippocampus, the amygdala, and the prefrontal cortex, benefit from meditation, according to research. Meditation restores the psyche of abuse victims. It restores the brain and enables the individual to respond to life from a place of empowerment rather than trauma.

Daily meditation practice strengthens neural pathways and increases grey matter density in brain regions associated with the fight-or-flight response and emotion regulation. Meditation also enables you to recognize your need to communicate with your abuser. When victims are unaware of this, they tend to make impulsive decisions that result in a return to the relationship. Additionally, it heightens your awareness of your emotions in general.

Support Yourself

In general, survivors of emotional abuse have been led to believe that they imagined the abuse they were experiencing. It is crucial that you begin to ground yourself in the reality that you were abused, but are no longer in an abusive situation. It is common for abuse victims to romanticize the relationship they were in and dwell on what might have been if they had been able to satisfy their partner. When contending with conflicting feelings towards an abuser, it is also helpful to connect with reality. As mentioned, one of the narcissist's strategies is to display and withdraw affection, and it is the affectionate side of the narcissist that attracts victims. The narcissist attempts to erode the victim's connection to reality, but once reconnected, the victim is able to see the abuser for who he truly is.

When survivors leave an abusive relationship, they are extremely vulnerable; their perpetrators will display their loving and affectionate side to manipulate them into returning. Therefore, it is imperative that you block all phone calls, texts, and other forms of communication so that he cannot enter your mind. This allows you to connect with what actually occurred, rather than allowing him to persuade you that your account of events is false.

Create an inventory of ten of the most abusive incidents that occurred during your relationship to begin the anchoring process. When you are compelled to reconnect with your abuser, read this list to remind yourself of how he degraded you and made you feel less than human. You can also jot down how he made you feel, such as "My abuser made me feel worthless." "My abuser caused me to feel depressed," "My abuser caused me to feel stupid." My abuser made me believe that I was receiving what I deserved and that no one could ever love me as he did.

Remind yourself of these emotions whenever you are tempted to pick up the phone and contact him or visit his home. Consider whether it feels nice for someone to convince you of something about yourself. The more you recall the negative emotions associated with the relationship, the simpler it will be to distance yourself from it.

Self-Soothing Work With Your Inner Child

You did not stumble into an abusive relationship by chance; rather, you have a history of childhood-rooted issues that have led you to this point. You will discover through therapy that certain fundamental requirements were not met during childhood. You settled for an abusive relationship in an attempt to replace that void. Once you have identified the vacuum, it is imperative that you learn how to fill it so that you do not leave yourself vulnerable to another abusive relationship. Because of what you endured as a child, you will need to be extremely compassionate with yourself during the healing process, as the abuse you endured was not your responsibility. Abuse has the ability to reopen ancient, never-healed wounds.

Your belief that you've never felt good enough has always been an integral part of your psyche. Your abusive partner merely confirmed what you've always believed to be true. When you are healing, it is crucial that you alter the narrative that is playing out in your consciousness. This is important in general, but it is especially crucial when you are recovering from abuse. Self-compassion can be the most effective form of compassion; therefore, it is crucial that you are kind to yourself during this time.

When you begin to experience these negative emotions, console yourself as if you were speaking to a bullied child on the playground. Tell yourself that you are the exact opposite of what your negative self-talk is attempting to convince you of. You can say things like, "I am worthy of love," "I am special," and "I deserve great things to happen in my life." You will eventually learn to stop blaming yourself and begin to surmount the toxic shame you have been exposed to. When you judge yourself for what has occurred, you are more likely to engage in self-destructive actions. You can overcome this by showing yourself compassion and reminding yourself that you are deserving of kindness and self-care.

Exercise

Whether it's taking long, intense walks, jogging, taking a dance class, or joining a gym, incorporating daily exercise into your regimen will aid in the healing process. If you lack motivation, don't attempt to do too much at once; for instance, you can begin with a ten-minute walk and gradually increase it over time. Exercise decreases cortisol levels and releases endorphins, which helps to replace the biochemical dependency you developed with your abuser. Chemicals such as cortisol, dopamine, serotonin, and adrenaline, which strengthen the bond with the abuser and create the cycle of highs and lows, contributed to the development of this addiction. After leaving an abuser, exercise permits you to build a wall of strength and resilience. It also helps to eliminate many of the physical problems associated with substance addiction, such as weight gain, sleep disturbances, accelerated aging, and a weakened immune system.

Put Unhealthy Coping Methods to Sleep

You did everything in your power to keep your narcissistic companion content and prevent him from exploding in rage. You spent your days walking on eggshells; you learned to be quiet and submissive, to doubt your every action, and to begin every conversation with "I'm sorry." You became skilled at dodging bullets, avoiding landmines, and acting as if portions of your ambitions, desires, and needs did not exist. You learned how to devalue yourself and accept completely abhorrent treatment from another human being. The mental anguish you had to endure in order to experience even a small amount of serenity and protect yourself and possibly your children was astounding. All of these terrible things you had to learn were not only unhealthy, but they are also not skills that will serve you well in a healthy relationship; therefore, you must develop new, healthy behaviors that will benefit you in a healthy relationship. There are two categories of self-monitoring involved in unlearning old habits: qualitative and quantitative.

Qualitative Monitoring entails being aware of the old behaviors you are engaging in, including how they manifest and how they make you feel.

Quantitative Monitoring entails keeping track of the frequency with which you engage in destructive behaviors by tallying the number of times you engage in them throughout the day.

Although both forms of self-monitoring are effective, quantitative monitoring is the most advantageous because for the first time you can accurately measure your behavior and the triggers that cause bad habits to resurface. Previously, you may have had a vague idea of how severe your problem was, but now you can see it for yourself and have a means of gauging your progress.

Establishing a system for the self-monitoring process is essential. It should include what is being monitored, how observations will be recorded, and the frequency of the monitoring process. For instance, normalizing the abuse is one of the most prevalent coping strategies for women in abusive relationships. They do this by persuading themselves that they deserve the treatment or by claiming that other women experience the same thing, so it must be what males do. It is impossible to monitor each and every one of your thoughts, and sometimes you are unaware that you are thinking in this manner. However, there will be instances in which you will stop yourself, at which point you should record the information. This process does not need to be intricate; simply carry a notebook with you and jot down the relevant information. If you realize that something prompted you to begin thinking in this manner, record that as well. Record the date, the time, the thought, the stimulus, and how you felt when you began to have these thoughts.

Discover to Love Yourself

This may sound trite, but it is necessary if you want to move on with your life and eventually form a healthy relationship. When one loves oneself, he or she knows who they are and what they stand for. It is impossible for anyone to attempt to convince you that you are not the greatest! When you achieve a certain level of confidence and self-worth, you cannot be shaken by anything. Here are some suggestions on how to appreciate yourself after a relationship of abuse.

Get in Shape: When you appear good, you feel good! The benefits of exercise have already been discussed, so appearing good is merely a bonus. Choose not only to enhance your health, but also to transform your body. Aim for your ideal weight and physique, whatever they may be.

Once you have reached your optimal body shape, you should purchase new clothing. You don't need to spend a fortune, but you should invest in a few signature items that will make you feel great about yourself.

Have Fun Alone: Take one day out of the week to engage in an activity you enjoy. Many victims of abuse have difficulty being alone, which makes them easy prey for perpetrators. Time spent alone will teach you how to appreciate your own company. You could go to the cinema, eat out, or discover a new hobby, among other activities.

Try Something Different: Do things that you normally wouldn't. Try something daring and novel, such as skydiving or bungee leaping. You know yourself better than anyone else, so you can choose something that will add an element of surprise to your existence.

Even if it's not a regular occurrence, you should take a vacation somewhere. Visit a country that is outside of your comfort zone. If you lack the courage to travel alone, invite a friend. Experience a new culture, cuisine, and activities, while having fun.

Keeping a journal is an effective method for releasing negative emotions. It is also useful for monitoring your progress. When leaving an abusive relationship, you will experience more bad days than positive ones. Some days will be better than others, but after a while you will observe that your emotions are beginning to stabilize.

Learn to Say No: For women in abusive relationships, submission is a survival mechanism. You would never say no to your partner for dread of the consequences. However, now that you are no longer in an abusive relationship, it is essential that you do not transfer this submissive nature into your friendships or feel compelled to say yes to everyone. This will deplete your energy and personal time.

Regardless of how minor you believe the accomplishment to be, you should celebrate it. It is an accomplishment to go an entire day without thinking about your ex, and it is also an accomplishment to be consistent with your daily exercise routine. Pay close attention to these details and reward yourself accordingly.

Provoke Yourself: Is there something you have always desired to do but have never done? Create a list of these tasks and begin performing them. You may have always desired to participate in a triathlon or earn additional credentials. Determine that whatever you set your mind to, you will accomplish.

Learn to Trust Yourself: Before you entered an abusive relationship, your intuition warned you that something was amiss, but you chose to ignore them in the hope that things would improve. Familiarize yourself with that sensation, as you will experience it whenever something is wrong, and not just in relationships, but in all aspects of your life.

Avoid Displays of Weakness

In situations where it is impossible to completely avoid contact with a narcissist, you can protect yourself by establishing and maintaining clear boundaries. As you may well be aware, narcissists lack boundaries and dislike it when others place limits on their intrusions. However, if you adhere to them, they have little choice but to embrace them. Here are some guidelines for setting limits with narcissists.

Know Your Boundaries

Narcissists are frequently impolite and aggressive. Especially if you do not leap when they tell you to, they will call you names and harass you. Tell them if you will not tolerate name-calling, bullying, or disrespect. For instance, if they are misbehaving during a conversation, you could say, "Listen, if you continue to act this way, I will end this conversation until you are capable of showing me respect." You are not required to provide an explanation or rationale. If they continue to not take you seriously, say, "As I previously stated, your rudeness is unacceptable, and I am not willing to speak with you when you behave in this manner. Goodbye." Either disconnect the phone or leave the room. Do not engage them in further conversation and do not permit them to respond. The quicker and more decisively you act, the simpler it will be to disarm the narcissist.

The narcissist will likely continue their abusive behavior. They may attempt to contact you or follow you in an effort to persuade you that you are being unfair or excessive. They will use a variety of tactics to attempt to confound, intimidate, or make you feel guilty about your decision.

Although their pleading and the pressure they are applying are unsettling, you will not negotiate your boundaries. You'll feel stronger, less burdened, safer, and more tranquil if you stick to your decision.

Have an Evasion Strategy

You do not need another person's permission to exit an unhealthy interaction. You can exit a conversation using a variety of strategies. For instance, you can glance at your watch and exclaim, "Oh my goodness, it's time for me to leave!" Then depart.

What you claim to be tardy for is irrelevant. Every minute you allow a narcissist to torment you is another minute you give them access to your mind.

Alternately, you can glance at your phone and say, "I'm truly sorry, but I need to take an important call." This can be completed regardless of whether your phone is buzzing.

Or, since you already know the narcissist's personality, set an alarm on your phone in advance and excuse yourself when the alarm goes off.

You Determine What You Will Discuss

Politicians are skilled at this. Rarely do they respond to the query being asked during interviews. They speak about whatever interests them. Similarly, if a narcissist poses you an uncomfortable question, you should change the subject. Why put yourself through that again if they have a poor habit of criticizing you for how you spend your money or conduct yourself in a relationship when they inquire about your relationship or financial situation? Instead, alter the subject to something you know the narcissist enjoys talking about. For instance, you could ask them how they learned to manage their finances so well or if they have discovered the key to the ideal relationship. Even though they will now spend your time talking about themselves, you are no longer the focus of the conversation.

Limit the amount of personal information you disclose to a narcissist. They have less ammunition against you the less they know about you. If they have something negative to say about what you're doing, respond, "I am confident in the decisions I've made." Or, "I have taken note of your opinion."

Specify What They Are Doing

Narcissists are always attempting to see how far they can stretch the boundaries of a relationship. They desire to always be the center of attention. One method to stop this is to say, "I've noticed that whenever I begin talking about myself, you interrupt me to talk about yourself." Or, "That sounded like you were trying to put me down." After that, you don't need to say anything else; just state the facts and move on. What they say next is unimportant. You have left your mark on the discourse by revealing that you are aware of their activities.

Remove Attention From Them

Narcissists thrive on attention; they adore being complimented, admired, and lauded. When engaging in discourse with them, they ensure that they are the focal point. What you are experiencing, sensing, or feeling is irrelevant to them. Their current beliefs, statements, or needs are their top priority, and they expect you to concur with them. Perform periodic mental checks when communicating with a narcissist to avoid being carried away by their influence. Take note of your thoughts, feelings, and desires. If you find it difficult to do so in the moment, review the conversation after you have departed and recall your thoughts and feelings at the time. When you are aware of what is occurring, the narcissist's ability to suffocate you with their agenda is diminished. Attending a self-help group will expose you to the term "gray rock" when referring to narcissists. This requires limiting the degree to which you allow yourself to care for a narcissist. For the duration of your time with them, become impregnable as a rock. This is a method of dissociation in an emotionally dangerous environment. The gray rock approach is a reminder that you will not give them your energy or completely engage with them; you reserve this type of normal behavior for trustworthy individuals. Reacting emotionally or demonstrating vulnerability in the presence of a narcissist gives them permission to continue abusing you.

Narcissists relish eliciting an emotional response from others; in their perverted minds, it validates their existence. By demonstrating their influence over you, you encourage their unwelcome intrusions and undesirable behaviors. Obviously, narcissists are experts at getting others to respond to their folly, so there will be times when you fail despite your best efforts. However, when you realize it, alter the subject or apologize.

Realize You Will Need to Constantly Set Boundaries with a Narcissist

In the majority of situations, when dealing with normal individuals, you only need to establish boundaries once, and they will adhere to them. This does not apply to narcissists. They will persistently test the boundaries you establish in an effort to wear you down. Therefore, you must continually reestablish these boundaries if you wish to maintain them.

Don't Be So Critical of Yourself

If you fail to establish healthy boundaries or occasionally trip up, do not be too hard on yourself. Narcissists are highly skilled individuals, and in most cases, you have been interacting with this person for years before deciding to stand your ground. In such circumstances, you will have years of vulnerability to overcome, which is a significant obstacle. Allow yourself room for error, and when you recognize you've made a mistake, consider what you'll do differently the next time.

Concentrate on Enhancing Yourself

Narcissists are concerned with their appearance and image, so they expect those with whom they interact to validate them, typically at your expense. You must determine who you will be around a narcissist; ask yourself, "Do I want to feel strong and confident?" Or overpowered and diminutive?

What am I currently standing for?

How can I accord myself the highest regard in this circumstance?

The responses you provide will provide you with crucial insight into the person you aspire to be at that time.

Remember With Whom You Are Dealing

Underneath their phony exterior, narcissists are extremely insecure and void of self-worth. They have constructed a wall of confidence to conceal their true emotions from the rest of the world. When you know the truth about a narcissist, you can see them for who they truly are, as opposed to a tyrant who believes they know everything and has the ability to reduce you to a whimpering child. Remind yourself that the narcissist has a difficult existence, and that their constant need for approval must be exhausting. In no way am I implying that their problems justify their controlling and abusive behavior, but it does serve as a reminder to not take what they do personally and to have some compassion for them.

Implement the Consequences

If the narcissist does not respect your boundaries, you will need to implement consequences. This is the only method to convince them of your seriousness. Before meeting with a narcissist, determine what will happen if your boundaries are disregarded or violated. You do not want to be in the midst of a situation when you attempt to calculate the potential consequences. Once you have communicated the consequences to the narcissist, implement them promptly, without explanation, and without wasting any time. If you do not enforce them, you will reap the consequences, which is playing the narcissist's game.

When you begin to establish limits, narcissists will escalate their attacks. They may threaten to disown you or begin circulating rumors and gossip about you. This is the risk you assume by allowing a narcissist into your existence. You will also need to consider these potential outcomes that your boundaries may produce. You may need to pick your conflicts carefully in order to avoid making them so angry that they have a personal vendetta against you.

The Effects Of Having Narcissistic Parents As A Child

Imagine a woman who appears to be the perfect parent in public, but who yells and rages at her children and husband when they displease her at home... or a parent who intentionally confuses his children by telling them something didn't happen when it did, discrediting their experience and teaching them not to trust themselves...

These are both examples of parents who display narcissistic traits. As is the case with many other personality traits, narcissism is typically distributed across the population, with the majority of individuals falling somewhere in the middle of the spectrum and only a few reaching the extremes. Pathological narcissism, as exemplified by Narcissistic Personality Disorder (NPD), is uncommon, afflicting less than 1 percent of the population.

Typically, a person with Narcissistic Personality Disorder (NPD) will;
Possess an inflated sense of self-importance
Possess a sense of entitlement and anticipate continuous and excessive adulation.
Expect to be regarded as superior despite lacking the meritorious achievements
Exaggerate their achievements and abilities
Consider thoughts of wealth, authority, attractiveness, brilliance, and the ideal relationship.
Monopolise dialogues

They demean or look down on those they perceive to be inferior.
Expect preferential treatment and mindless submission to their demands.

Utilize others to accomplish your own objectives
Are unable or unwilling to acknowledge the demands and emotions of others. Consider that others are envious of you and be envious of others.

Behave in a manner that is arrogant or haughty, appearing ostentatious, boastful, or pretentious.
Insist on obtaining the best of everything, such as the best car or office.

Narcissists have difficulty dealing with anything that is perceived as criticism or that penetrates the image they have constructed of themselves. When this occurs, individuals may become enraged, insult others, struggle to control their emotions, and experience repressed feelings of remorse, vulnerability, and humiliation.

Being Raised By A Narcissistic Parent

Being reared by a narcissistic parent produces the belief that "I am not good enough." Typically, narcissistic parents have a possessive relationship with their young children. Their children are perceived as an extension of themselves and serve as a source of self-esteem for the parent; "look at how wonderful my children are, didn't I do a great job?"

The minors are utilized to attract the attention of others. The children learn to conform to the molds that their parents create for them, which may lead to anxiety for the child who continually sacrifices his or her individuality to please the parent.

In order for their life to remain stable, the child of a narcissistic parent must concur with the parent's agenda. The expression of their own emotions or opinions may result in conflicts with their parents, which may involve anger, weeping, or discipline. This teaches the child that his or her emotions and viewpoints are insignificant, invalid, and irrelevant, and as a result, he or she will frequently suppress their own feelings in order to maintain domestic harmony.

Not all narcissists are malicious. They are frequently kind, but this compassion is almost always contingent on certain conditions. Frequently, the child will realize that their parent's generosity causes them to feel indebted to them. The sentiment "If I do this for you, you owe me" is always implicit or explicit in acts of kindness. Kindness and affection are subject to conditions.

The behavior of a narcissist can be difficult to tolerate at the best of times, but for a child, it can be shocking and upsetting. Young children cannot simply abandon their family, so they cultivate hope by sacrificing their self-respect and placing the blame on themselves.

The child internalizes the notion that he or she is the problem: "If I were better at this or that, my parents would love me more." The parent's belief that he or she is the ideal parent perpetuates this myth because the parent believes that any resistance or negativity from the child is the child's fault.

The difficulty of growing up with a narcissistic parent is that the child typically does not recognize that anything is amiss. When we are young, we are only exposed to what our families expose us to. Often, it is not until the child is an adult that they begin to make meaning of their childhood. This realization is frequently aided by a friend or companion who recognizes the narcissist's peculiar or bizarre parenting style.

Characteristics of Adult Children of Narcissists

1. Uncertainty and Guilt

Adult offspring of narcissistic parents fear that doing what is best for themselves will harm others. They have been 'trained' to prioritize their parents' requirements, making it difficult for them to prioritize their own without feeling selfish. This indecision and remorse can be permanently paralyzing.

Internalization of Gaslighting

Gaslighting is a form of psychological manipulation in which an individual or group subtly sows seeds of doubt in a target, causing them to dispute their own memory, perception, or judgment.

The adult offspring of a narcissistic parent may feel they have little to offer, despite the fact that the opposite may be true. Growing up, their talents and abilities may have been minimized, ignored, or co-opted by narcissistic parents who felt threatened by their children's abilities.

Even when adults achieve success, they may believe they do not deserve it, which can lead to imposter syndrome.

3) Love and Devotion

Even after growing up surrounded by lies, manipulation, and abuse, it may be exceedingly challenging for adult children of narcissists to stop caring about and adoring their parent. They may even engage in relationships with narcissistic individuals if they experience remorse for attempting to distance themselves or establish boundaries. A love based on manipulations and circumstances is something they are accustomed to, whereas an unconditional love may seem extremely menacing.

4) Resilience and Strength

Very often, adult children of narcissistic parents exhibit a remarkable capacity for expressing compassion and love for others, are able to form meaningful relationships, and learn to love and care for themselves. It is possible to recover from having a narcissistic parent as a child, as will be discussed later in this essay.

5) Persistent Self-blame

Whether or not the parent is publicly abusive to the child, they are almost always emotionally tone-deaf and too preoccupied with their own problems to hear their child's distress. As previously mentioned, in an effort to preserve the family unit, the child (even if they are now an adult) avoids criticizing their parent and instead places all the blame on themselves: "If I had been better at...", "If I hadn't been such a difficult child..." etc.

This may persist into maturity, with the adult child continuing to take responsibility for things that are not necessarily their fault. In numerous instances, they are made the scapegoat in order to preserve harmony.

6) Echoism

Echoists and Narcissists are complementary, and you can learn more about Echoism on this page. Essentially, narcissistic parents may spontaneously erupt in rage or shed tears, compelling their children to occupy as little space as possible to avoid provoking one of these emotional eruptions. It may appear as if they are traveling on eggshells in order to prevent their parent from having a tantrum.

7) Uncertain Attachment

Adult children of narcissists are likely to develop an insecure attachment to their parents, as they never experience a secure base from which they can confidently explore their surroundings.

A parent's neglect, manipulation, or emotional absence may cause their child to fear how safe they will feel in the care of others. This causes some individuals to become fiercely independent, believing that they cannot rely on anyone else. However, it may cause some to adhere to their relationships for affection and constantly seek their partner's attention.

8) Parental Parent

Children who grow up with a narcissistic parent will have planned their entire life and personality around their parent's happiness, and will go on to structure their lives around the happiness of others, with many of them entering the nurturing professions.

How to Proceed Forward

After having been reared by a narcissistic parent, there are a number of different ways to recover. It is up to you whether you choose to engage in a therapy partnership or go through your recovery with a partner. Working through this healing process with another family member could result in complications; proceed with caution.

Here are some essential steps you can take to initiate the healing process:

1) Recognise. The initial step in everything is awareness. We cannot proceed until we understand the source of our suffering. If you believe that one of your parents has narcissistic tendencies or Narcissistic Personality Disorder, you are likely reading this page.

2) Study. Inform yourself about NPD and its potential effects on the family structure. Internet searches, textbooks, and conversations with clinicians who comprehend narcissism are essential.

3) Recount your experiences. This exercise may be difficult; therefore, I strongly advise you to seek assistance. For each sign and symptom of NPD, recall and record your own childhood or adulthood experiences that correspond.

For each of these recollections, the narrative must be retold with the new dialogue, "My parent is a narcissist and is treating me this way because of that." There is no remorse in this new conversation; neither for you nor your parent. This is a method for reframing one's experiences in light of new information and releasing oneself from remorse.

4) Identify. During the antecedent phase, it is possible that the narcissistic parent's abusive, traumatic, and negligent behavior becomes apparent. You will likely be able to identify emotional abuse and neglect (guilt-

tripping, manipulation), as well as psychological abuse (gaslighting or the silent treatment), as awful as it may be. You may also find instances of physical and financial maltreatment (neglect or excessive gift-giving).

5) Grieve. There may be a great deal of sorrow involved in this method of rehabilitation. Both mourning for the upbringing you never had and lamenting the shattered image of your parent. As stated, as children we only know what we know. Consequently, as you get older and realize that other children had a completely different upbringing than you did, you may feel resentful, cheated, and disappointed that you were deprived of this opportunity.

You may have grown up protecting or idolizing your parents, only to discover that they have caused you significant harm. This may be quite destabilizing, and we may discover that we need to grieve for the image of our parents that we once held.

6) Progress through the phases of development. There is a good chance that you overlooked some crucial developmental stages as a child, and now is the time to begin experiencing and mastering them. Now is the time to investigate your own identity, to experiment with your sexuality and dating, and to determine what you want to study and what you want to achieve in life. You will likely need to learn to ask for what you need (you may begin by asking for directions), recognize your long-repressed emotions, and establish healthy boundaries.

7) Understand. Finally, it is essential to recognize and understand that your narcissistic parent will not change. Even if you confront them, or even if you want

to confront them, it is highly unlikely that they will change their methods.

As previously stated, confronting a narcissistic parent can result in significant family conflict, as the narcissist will experience immense guilt and vulnerability when their perfect image is shattered. This may cause them to be extremely protective and enraged.

It is equally important to acknowledge and perhaps even forgive your other parent. It is likely that if one of your parents is a narcissist, the other is an enabler. Enablers normalize and perpetuate the narcissist's abusive behavior by accepting and/or condoning it.

Occasionally, enablers may aid narcissists in their vile work by tolerating and perpetuating their abuse. By denying the abuse and failing to protect their children from it, enablers become complicit, even if they are affected by it.

How to Deal with a Self-Centered Mother

It is difficult to live with a narcissistic mother. Narcissists are overly egocentric and frequently view their children as extensions of themselves. Frequently, a narcissistic parent leaves their child feeling ignored, unimportant, and exploited.

What Self-Centered Mothers Do

If your mother is a narcissist, she may appear selfless, as if she is continuously doing things for her children and never considering herself.

A narcissistic mother may serve as a soccer coach, PTO president, or class parent. Such participation is, however, self-serving. She does it because she needs to be involved in every decision and desires attention.

She may be unduly interested in your life if you are an adult. She could make your actions about her more than about you. Perhaps you are planning a wedding, but she refuses to attend if your father is present. Or, when you speak, she continually shifts the focus back to herself. If you have children, she may exert great effort to become your co-parent, even if it means alienating the other parent.

If your mother is a narcissist, she might be emotionally manipulative and authoritative. It is possible for narcissistic parents to provide excessively positive feedback that rapidly morphs into excessively harsh or punitive criticism.

Your mother may not see you for who you truly are, only as an extension of herself. She may have difficulty comprehending and accepting your emotions, becoming frightened or enraged when she perceives rejection or derision.

Identifying a Narcissist

Your mother may have a few, such as self-centeredness and a sense of entitlement. Or she may have a severe case of narcissistic personality disorder (NPD).

Among the symptoms of narcissistic personality disorder are:

A strong sense of grandiosity (high levels of self-esteem, self-importance, self-confidence, and superiority complex)
Insolent attitude or behavior
Taking advantage of others in order to obtain what they want
The belief that one is unique or exceptional
Exaggerating abilities and accomplishments
Excessive desire for acclaim
Feeling or believing that others are envious of them
Lack of compassion

Visions of brilliance, authority, or achievement

Sense of entitlement (they believe they merit special treatment because of who they are).

How to Deal with a Narcissistic Mother

If your mother is a narcissist, you can manage your relationship in the following ways:

Set limits. Create and uphold healthy boundaries. Be clear about what is acceptable and what is not.

Stay tranquil. Even if she insults you, avoid responding emotionally to her words. "The narcissist wants a response from you to demonstrate their power and ability to manipulate your mood," Chandy explains. "Your peace is your strength."

Plan your responses. "Have a respectful exit strategy when conversations go off the rails," advises Perlin. Prepare and rehearse responses such as "I have to go, Mom" and "We'll just have to agree to disagree."

Let go. You may experience pressure to make your mother happy and to be a good child. Abandon these notions. Remember that it is not your responsibility to make your mother feel special, desired, or essential.

Obtain assistance. Consult a counselor. They may assist you in comprehending how her narcissism affects you and in learning how to end the pattern.

Step aside. It may be prudent to have minimal or no contact with your mother, especially if she is violent or aggressive. Instead, focus on the things you can influence. "I no longer communicate with my family," Chandy explains. She believes this is the only method to deal with a narcissistic mother if your development and happiness are paramount.

What to Avoid Doing When Your Mother Is a Narcissist

If your mother is a narcissist, you should avoid the following:

Do not anticipate an apology. Narcissists are resistant to accept constructive criticism. Typically, they have justifications and explanations for their actions. Your mother may not recognize that she is wrong or that her actions are bad. She likely views herself as the victim, not you.

Do not try to heal or restore her. You cannot alter her character. Narcissists typically grew up with exploitative and abusive narcissistic parents. It is something she cannot control and from which she will likely never recover. It may be helpful to develop compassion for her struggles and acknowledge that her actions are not deliberate.

Chapter 5: Making Amends

Reconciling with oneself is the first step in forgiving others. However, you must first comprehend what it is to forgive and make restitution. When you absolve yourself, you can make wise decisions about whether or not to forgive your abuser (the narcissist) and you can understand what a genuine apology entails. It is in your best interest to absolve yourself before anyone else because during the abusive journey you endured, you may have dealt with inappropriate friendships, broken trust, or even lost yourself along the way. Part of forgiving yourself is letting go of the baggage and resentment you've accumulated throughout it all so that you can live a fulfilling and fruitful life. Here are a few suggestions on how to absolve yourself when you feel your worst and are overcome by shame:

Be conscious of your emotions.

Oftentimes, attempts to forgive ourselves fail because we push away difficult emotions such as guilt, anger, sorrow, and shame. To genuinely absolve yourself for the burdens you have caused, you must process each emotion separately. Accept the feeling, experience the feeling, and then let it go.

Recognize your contrition

Uh oh! Did you make a mistake? Was it a major setback this time? Stop before you begin descending into a pit of shame and remorse. What have you learned from this error? Taking responsibility for one's actions can be facilitated by paying attention, recognizing one's errors, and then responding to them. It may also assist you in releasing the burden you carry on your shoulders or in your heart.

Consider your failures as opportunities for development

There is no success without failure, and there is no failure without success. Every opportunity for development is a learning curve, and none of us are flawless. Let go of what the narcissist says and begin to focus on how you truly feel. Now that you have made a grave error, there is nothing you can do about it. There is no greater level of abuse you will experience than when you focus on your own error. Utilize what you've learned and move on by not repeating the mistake.

Discuss with your inner critic

Writing in a journal is likely the simplest method to respond to one's inner critic. Write down what your mind is telling you, and then write a response to it while viewing it as if it were a letter from a friend. By doing so, you are teaching yourself how to recognize your thought patterns and locating the source of your self-sabotage. Additionally, use this time to create a list of all the things you are proud of about yourself, which will help boost your confidence when the dark days arrive.

Exhibit self-love

Self-love involves being aware of your flaws while focusing on your assets. It is about learning how to unconditionally embrace yourself for who you are. Therefore, based on your prior experiences, you may not have had the best of success learning how to love yourself. Don't let this discourage you or prevent you from being yourself. Be kind and compassionate to yourself, be patient with yourself and your emotions, and learn to ask for assistance when you need it. All of these involve loving yourself in such a manner that you will not require anyone else to do it for you.

Learning to forgive yourself is one thing, but must you also forgive the narcissist who placed you in a position where you must forgive yourself? These previous suggestions are applicable whenever you feel terrible for something, but forgiveness also involves forgiving others. Nevertheless, the issue remains: must you truly forgive the narcissist?

Before deciding to forgive (or not forgive), there are a few things to consider when pondering this question. All the scenarios depict what could occur if you ask the narcissist for absolution.

They may attempt to magnify your error into something much larger than you intended. The sensitivity of narcissists to criticism. So, according to their perspective, they did nothing wrong, whereas you are to blame for something that you may have viewed as innocuous or minor. In this case, the solution is to not seek absolution from a narcissist and, when accused, to recognize the situation for what it is, rather than allowing them to confuse you.

- Seeking forgiveness from a narcissist will result in them gaslighting you and placing more of the responsibility on you than on their own errors. They may accuse you of being excessively sensitive and make you feel guilty for requesting an apology in the first place.

The narcissist's perspective and interpretation of events may leave you confused and complicate the process of forgiving. For instance, your narcissistic friends (or the narcissist's friends) may be angry with you for not forgiving the individual for xxx reason. In this way, you may develop their perception of the situation, which causes self-doubt and a distortion of what is 'right' and 'wrong' in your mind and intuition.

To return to the original issue, can I forgive the narcissist? Forgiveness entails seeking or obtaining justice and ensuring that it is handled effectively. There is no true justice because narcissists cannot help being narcissistic due to the disorder they suffer from (whether intentionally or unintentionally). This suggests that neither forgiveness nor forgiveness is possible. Even though the individual with NPD has a disorder, they must still make decisions in every situation. What they choose to do is ultimately outside of your control and is not your responsibility. When anyone, narcissistic or not, chooses not to forgive or continues to make poor decisions, they are not attempting. Their apologies and actions may appear repetitive and caught in a perpetual loop. Yes, narcissists struggle with empathy and regret for their actions, but does that mean you should enable them? If you want to pardon them, you must first forgive yourself for enduring the relationship's pain before deciding to forgive them. If you are going to forgive them for all of their transgressions, do so discretely and privately; otherwise, conflict may ensue.

Apologies Apologies are intended to be sincere and genuine. Sincere apologies emanate from the heart and are accompanied by a great deal of thought, making them unique and sincere. To be genuinely apologetic, one must possess empathy, the capacity for sympathy, and a high degree of emotional intelligence. If you have ever sincerely apologized, you may have considered the situation and realized you were in the wrong. This exemplifies what it means to accept responsibility for one's actions. To be accountable, one must be able to completely acknowledge their errors, swallow their pride, and confess their wrongdoing. The narcissist lacks these characteristics, as well as the prerequisites for genuine contrition. Now that you understand forgiveness and why it may or may not be a good idea to forgive the narcissist, let's examine what false apologies are so that we can distinguish between fake and genuine condolences.

Developing Stable Relationships

Healthy relationships (friendships, marriages, colleague relationships, etc.) are the antithesis of what it is like to live with and be around a narcissist. It is when two individuals can reach an agreement and have a level of mutual respect that does not cross boundaries. As a consequence, this highlights the significance of trust, honesty, and support. A narcissist does not abide by the rules and has poor communication skills, both of which are essential for growing, developing, and enhancing healthy and supportive relationships. If you have endured an unhealthy narcissistic relationship with a family member or someone else, you may have been neglected and isolated, causing you to lose some companions. If this sounds familiar, the following advice will help you rebuild your relationships so you can live a happier existence surrounded by supportive people.

1. Implement a courteous and calm conversation

Before initiating a conversation, you must plan out what you will say. Consider the reasons why the friendship ended in the first place. Consider the wrongs you committed and the role you played in the dissolution of your relationship. After apologizing, you should only then proceed to determine what they did, as it is vital that they also be informed - assuming you have already done so. If they have blocked you and you are unable to text them, use a friend's phone or attempt to deliver a letter to their letterbox. For this phase, be concise: a brief hello, my name is xxx, and I would like to discuss xxx. Please call or email me. You need nothing more than a simple note that is brief, sweet, and to the point because you must now wait for their response.

2.Be absolutely certain of what you want

Once they have reached out to you again, be sure to be forthright, honest, and genuine about what you want from the interaction. Are we to be pals once more? Is it acceptable to be acquaintances while letting the past be the past? Whatever it is, ensure that you have thoroughly considered this.

3.Be sincerely truthful in a courteous manner

Throughout the conversation, the opposing party may also wish to discuss certain requirements. They will want to explain their perspective and how they feel. Ensure you listen attentively, focus on the smallest details, and continue to read their body language for clues as to whether you should respond. Ensure that during the interaction you are neither offensive nor defensive. Consider what you are doing and how you are feeling; if it cannot be rehashed, it may be best to accept this part, keep your lips shut, and move on. You at least attempted.

4.Resolve the issue

If you are attempting to rebuild, you should be aware of their concerns, emotions, desires, and requirements at this point in the conversation. Cooperatively attempt to resolve whatever the initial issue was. Make restitution by demonstrating how much you value your friendship and explaining how you will do better in the future. Also, request that they inform you of what you can continue to do.

5. Let go of perfectionism

Perfectionism is the desire and maintenance of total control. Have control over yourself and your emotions, but never over another individual or situation. Expect that the conversation will not end effortlessly or perfectly. Recognize that they may decline your offer to restart your relationship. Remember to take a step back and pay attention to your emotions and desired response when interacting with them.

6. Give a genuine apology

The topics of forgiveness and apologies were discussed. When you are apologizing, you should really focus on what you are regretful for. Are you regretful that the relationship ended due to xxx or your inappropriate behavior? Or do you regret not acting sooner when you ought to have? What lessons have you learnt from this error? Most people find it difficult to forgive, but if you have properly forgiven yourself, their response will not matter because you have already granted yourself genuine absolution and can only improve yourself.

7.Be responsible

What did you precisely do? It is prudent to describe not only what you did, but also how you injured them and how you made them feel (preferably without them saying so). Expect nothing in return from them during this procedure. Simply explain to them what your primary responsibilities are. By doing so, you demonstrate authenticity and the capacity or desire to improve.

8.Think positive thoughts

When you are fixated on negativity, you will receive negativity. Make sure you are in a good mood and your thoughts about the outcome are set to auto-positive before engaging in the conversation. When you enter a conversation with a positive outlook, it can alter the entire dynamic of the interaction; this demonstrates your confidence, and the other party will follow your lead.

9. Create wholesome limits

While offering your contrition and working with the other party to determine how to make amends and move forward, don't lose sight of your own morals. Consider what you believe in first and foremost. Regardless of how badly you've erred, you shouldn't completely relax your guard due to the vulnerability you're creating. Remember to remind them at some point that you still stand for your own beliefs and would not want them to be violated.

10. Aim for both of your objectives.

Remember why you are conversing with your friend: to reestablish and strengthen your relationship. The purpose or result of your interaction is to apologize while solving your problems, listening to their desires and needs, and maintaining your boundaries. If the conversation is going well, feel free to invite them out again and continue strengthening your relationship.

11. Learn how to bid farewell

You may encounter individuals with whom you simply cannot get along or who were intended to be in your life only as a lesson or for a brief period of time. Accept that you cannot perfect every relationship you have and be willing to part ways if necessary. Moreover, if the person continues to be negative or hostile, these are the individuals you are trying to avoid in the first place, and it may be for the best in the long run.

Rebuilding a relationship and bringing it back together involves both parties, not just you. Healthy relationships are characterized by communication, compromise, sacrifice, and a willingness to "agree to disagree." If these elements are present in your supportive relationships, then a friendship, family relationship, or long-term partner (or whatever you desire from it) will be most beneficial for both parties. Alternatively, if your relationship cannot be rekindled, the learning experience of it is how you move on and progress in life while simultaneously closing this chapter of your relationship with healthy closure.

How to Bid Farewell to a Narcissist

At this point, you should be aware of any narcissists in your life or within your family. You should also have realized by this point that attempting to make apologies with a narcissist is likely to fail. It is difficult to say farewell to anyone, let alone a family member, who has wronged you, but the point is that everyone must accept responsibility for their actions. Everyone on the planet has options and decisions from which to choose, including narcissists, whether or not their disorder controls them. You may have approached your narcissistic mother or sibling and attempted to explain the consequences of their actions, or you may have repeatedly attempted to share your success with them. Doesn't the result always remain the same? The narcissist will either steal your limelight by returning the conversation to themselves, use you for something, or charm you out of your 'insensitivity' and 'criticism,' at least in their eyes. Take a moment to consider life without them, regardless of how difficult it may be to do so. Imagine the independence. Consider how little control and influence they will have over you. Imagine having the freedom to make your own choices, etc. Imagine a life in which you can do whatever you want in the 'right' manner. Cutting ties with your narcissistic family members will be more beneficial to you than to them. Yes, they may mourn you, but only because you have been their victim for years. Yes, they may attempt to reintegrate you into their lives by hoovering, but how much energy are you willing to continue to invest in their behavior? When separating from a narcissist, it is essential to recognize that they are inherently lacking in empathy. It's not that they intend to be this way, but it's inherent in their essence. Yes, they can change, but it requires commitment, patience, and effort that will not be resolved in a few brief years.

When leaving a narcissistic family member behind, the greatest dread appears to be having the freedom to make your own decisions and stand on your own. You may have depended on and served your narcissistic parent or grandparent for a very long time, but the reality is that they will continue to hold you responsible for everything that is not your responsibility. Your self-esteem and mental health will continue to decline, and it will become increasingly difficult to break the cycle in the future. In all honesty, you know what it's like to grow up in a narcissistic home; you are familiar with the anguish and victimization that accompany being a part of the environment. When we have children and establish our own families, we frequently repeat history by teaching our offspring based on our own experiences. If you don't break the cycle of narcissism now, it will only continue to grow. Now is the time to improve your health and learn how to surmount your ingrained childhood patterns. Now is the time to seek assistance through counseling or social gatherings. This will help you plan for the future so that you can live a long, fulfilling life filled with numerous close friendships.

When you sense the urge to contact a family member, think before acting. Why are you extending yourself? Do you wish to impart your knowledge? Do you wish to impart your knowledge? Do you wish to persuade them to seek assistance so that you no longer have to remain away? Remind yourself that despite all your efforts and desires, the narcissist will never accept responsibility. Yes, they may claim they will take action, but only to lure you back in. Recall the maltreatment and manipulation techniques that have caused your mental health to deteriorate and your cycles to repeat. Say one thing: "It is not my responsibility to help them understand the long-term consequences of their actions." Narcissists will waste your time (if you haven't already noticed) trying to justify their apologies by making excuses for their actions, actions that will not alter in the end. If you sever ties with them now, it may be enough for them to get the assistance they need (crossing fingers), and you can return to share your experiences apart later in life. As you mature and begin standing up for yourself and acquiring mental strength through personal development, you may discover that working towards something is more satisfying than being manipulated to get what you want. It's time to own who you are, dream large, and propel yourself forward in life by making your own decisions.

Learning to recover from a loss

Intentionally severing ties with a narcissist is one thing, but actually doing so is an entirely different challenge. There will be times when you want to reach out to them, and other times when you simply want to silently reflect on the happy times you shared with them. You may even question if they occasionally consider you as much as you consider them. As a narcissist lacks empathy and emotional control, it is unlikely that they will mourn you or think about you as frequently as you would like. This should be sufficient to convince you that you deserve better. Severing connections is inevitable under all circumstances. Eventually, you will want to extend your wings and break free from the narcissist's suffocating grasp, regardless of whether you choose to forgive or attempt to mend the relationship. Here are some recommendations on how to heal from your relationship and achieve closure.

1. Write a closure letter

The letter of farewell should be primarily addressed to you. It will assist you in processing your emotions and saying what needs to be said without actually speaking to them. It aids in forgiving what occurred and increases one's self-respect. You can choose to send the letter, but it would be more advantageous to keep it to yourself, as the narcissist will likely view it as an invitation to commit additional offenses. You should write the letter solely for your own benefit, so that you can obtain acceptance and closure regarding the relationship.

2. Express your feelings

In a cloud of confusion, you may feel rejected, responsible, sad, lonely, furious, relieved, or all of the above. To completely accept that your relationship has ended, it is best to experience each emotion separately. Cry if you must, get furious if you must, and sit alone to process in order to advance your development. You can organize your memories by placing photographs, objects, and a playlist of songs in a box. Examine each item with care, and reminisce when necessary. When you are prepared, you can return it or give it away. For the time being, it may make you feel better to retain it so you can retrieve it and process your emotions as you recall your times together.

3.Plan a closure ritual

Every relationship, regardless of its health, is symbolic. Creating a ceremony for forgiveness and farewells can help you understand that your relationships have been severed. To relieve the negative energy, locate something they gave you and shred or donate it. Or, if that is too challenging, locate something that reminds you of them, such as a song or a poem, and transform the lyrics or verses into a setting for closure. Releasing the negative energy you have been holding onto will assist you in breaking out of your rut and getting back into the game of personal development.

4. Fill in the gap

When we lose something, we typically feel void and dissatisfied. We feel alone and somewhat damaged. The narcissist was your addiction, and you must now replace the void by substituting a positive addiction in its place. For instance, if you recently stopped smoking, you will need a replacement habit. Every time you have a craving for nicotine, you may choose to go for a run or be creative in order to avoid smoking. Similarly, you can fill the vacancy left by the narcissist. Be adaptable to change and view this new experience as a chance to improve your life.

5. Prepare for the future

Typically, the narcissist will eventually reach out to you. If they are family, you may not be able to avoid bumping into them or seeing them during the holidays. However, creating a plan for when these situations occur can force you to leave your comfort zone. Write down brief reminders of why you are severing ties. Write down everything they did or how your relationship was dysfunctional; make a mental note of where your life was going with them versus where it is going now. That way when you do run into them or have to talk to them, you can stand strong and have the courage to still walk away.

6. Be tolerant of the suffering

The first step in releasing the anguish and emptiness in your heart is to acknowledge and accept your emotions. Also recognize that these emotions will not last eternally. Recognize that it is difficult now, but that everything you are attempting to do will improve and become simpler as time passes. Be patient with your emotions, as avoiding them will only make them worse and increase the volume of your inner critic. The inner critic is an unhelpful voice that constantly reminds you of your flaws. You have just escaped a narcissist; there is no need for your psyche to be one as well. So be patient and learn that it is okay to feel as you do in this moment.

This is arguably the most essential stage. Taking something personal implies that you continue to bear the burdens that the narcissist imposed on you. You must remember that you are not responsible for their decisions, actions, behaviors, or way of life. It was never. Their flaws and shortcomings are and have never been your challenges. Remember that the manner in which they live their lives and the opinions they hold have nothing to do with you. This form of thinking places the onus of responsibility on the individual. How much abuse are you willing to endure from yourself, let alone from others? Own who you are and never take the words or actions of others personally.

There are several factors to consider when saying goodbye to the one individual who may have been there for you at one point. You may have been taught that family should be there through thick and lean. Perhaps you were raised to never give up. However, you must ask yourself how much agony, suffering, and difficulty you are willing to endure before you completely lose control. Family is not synonymous with blood, and blood is not required for family. You deserve prosperity. You're worthy of loyalty. You deserve forgiveness and gratitude. You have the right to learn how to grant yourself this by gaining independence from the narcissistic relationship.

What Effect Does Narcissism Have On Your Relationship?

A narcissist's focus in a relationship is on themselves.

In psychological literature, the influence of narcissism on relationships is well-documented. Most individuals in a love relationship, especially a romantic one, embrace a degree of give-and-take. There is no giving with narcissists; their self-obsession means the entire relationship revolves around their desires or requirements. People associated with narcissists frequently exhibit physical and psychological signs of stress, or abandon them for their own safety. There is therapy for both parties, but for it to be effective, the narcissist must demonstrate a genuine desire to change.

Typically, narcissists are not engaged in long-term relationships.

Weak self-esteem is protected by an inflated sense of one's own importance, and narcissists are frequently convinced they are always right. They will do anything to obtain what they desire, regardless of the feelings of others.

People who are narcissistic may desire the attention they receive in new relationships.

Narcissism in romantic relationships can be destructive. Initially, narcissists tend to allure their partners, but later, more nefarious traits may emerge. They desire unconditional love on their terms and will withhold it when offended. They may seek out companions with similar abandonment phobias so that they will not leave them regardless of how terrible their behavior is. Individuals who feel threatened or apathetic may engage in substance abuse, promiscuity, and other self-soothing behaviors.

Narcissists are typically obsessed with themselves.

People with this abnormal mindset are typically not interested in forming long-term relationships. The effect of their narcissism on their relationships is a focus on short-term delight in the form of sexual dalliances, devoid of genuine connection. They view commitment as unimportant unless it is motivated by self-interest. They are restless and constantly seeking the next interaction. This causes anxiety and jealousy in their partners, who must then determine whether to leave or remain.

If other people do not follow their lead, narcissists are more prone to conflict.

One of the most obvious effects of narcissism on relationships is domestic violence, which occurs when narcissists physically or emotionally abuse their partners. Some narcissists use passive-aggressive tactics to undermine their partners' self-esteem, thereby preventing abandonment and bolstering their inflated sense of self. Due to the narcissist's abandonment issues, it is extremely dangerous for the victimized partner to leave a violent relationship.

A narcissist may be excessively competitive with their partner.

Children of narcissistic parents may not receive the affirmation they need to develop empathy for others, and as a result, they may become narcissists themselves. In contrast, some researchers believe that the self-esteem movement's exclusive emphasis on positive reinforcement may be to blame. The effects of narcissism on relationships can last a lifetime, but psychotherapy, cognitive behavioral therapy, and antidepressants for underlying depression are effective treatments. In order for therapy to be successful, the narcissist must be willing to transform.

Please be aware that narcissistic abuse is initially very, very subtle and progressively becomes more obvious. Accepting that they are in love with an illusion is one of the difficulties faced by individuals in such relationships. Regardless of how wonderful the relationship was in the beginning, if you are experiencing maltreatment, there is no turning back. You must separate yourself from the other person and initiate the self-love process. This is the narcissist's gift to you, provided you accept it.

It is not always simple to love someone with a narcissistic personality disorder. Narcissism is characterized by a need for others' approval and an impaired ability to discern the needs of others. The first step in seeking compassion and support for narcissists is recognizing and treating this disorder as a serious mental illness. With consistent, long-term care, narcissists and their loved ones can receive assistance.

Relationships with people who have narcissistic personality disorder (NPD) can be challenging. Narcissists typically have an inflated sense of ego and entitlement, put themselves first, lack empathy, and may engage in aggressive behavior towards others.

It is frequently difficult for narcissists to recognize the perverted and destructive patterns of their thoughts and actions. This may make receiving treatment challenging, though not impossible.

Only a professional evaluation can determine if a loved one has narcissistic personality disorder. After taking this initial difficult step and acknowledging that there is a problem, you and your partner may make progress toward an improved relationship.

NARCISSISTIC RELATIONSHIP PATTERN
Numerous narcissists are unable to accept themselves and others as whole, integrated beings with both positive and negative characteristics. Moreover, narcissists tend to perceive others as either ideal or flawed, depending on the treatment they receive. These characteristics manifest in three extremely regular patterns:

At the beginning of a relationship, for many, adoring a narcissist is relatively straightforward. Individuals with NPD may be alluring during the courtship phase due in part to their idealized view of the "perfect relationship." This may seem to you like the traditional honeymoon period that many young couples experience. However, for narcissists, this period is significantly more intense. It entails living out your romantic fantasies, exhibiting you and the rest of the world all of their fantastic qualities without revealing their weaknesses.

PHASE OF DECLINING IMPACT: Eventually, or sometimes overnight, the honeymoon phase ends. This is a time when a narcissist's aversion to vulnerability begins to surface, preventing the relationship from growing closer in terms of candor. Your partner begins to recognize your less-than-perfect qualities and may make frequent remarks about required adjustments. If you decline these recommendations, your companion will feel insulted. Because narcissists perceive any offense to themselves as a flaw in the behavior of others, they may begin to withdraw at this stage.

Many relationships with narcissists result in the disregard of the other partner. Even if they look back on the relationship with affection, narcissists rarely accept responsibility for how it ended. Occasionally, the partner may be the one to abandon a relationship involving abuse.

Even though this is a common pattern in relationships with narcissists, it is still possible to assist your loved one on the path to therapy.

LOVING A NARCISSIST

One of the most difficult aspects of adoring narcissists is their lack of empathy, which can make you feel as though they are not truly present even when they are with you. Individuals with NPD are incapable of understanding the emotions of others and frequently exploit others to fulfill their own desires, particularly their need for continuous adulation.

This lack of empathy may appear frigid and manipulative, but it is a symptom of severe mental illness and does not indicate malice on the part of your loved one. Learning how to empathize with narcissists without criticizing them is a crucial step in gaining their trust, which could make therapy simpler. Studies have shown that it is possible to reduce narcissistic tendencies and increase empathy among narcissists, although more research is needed on this topic.

Counseling may aid narcissists in recognizing the effects of NPD on their relationships and ultimately promote recovery. Narcissists require treatment because they are more prone than the general population to substance abuse, anxiety, mood, and personality disorders.

FINDING SUPPORT FOR YOURSELF
In a relationship with a narcissist, the risk of abuse is unquestionable. However, it may be difficult for the loved

ones of narcissists to distinguish between acceptance of NPD and tolerance of abusive behavior.

While it is beneficial to recognize that your loved one has a severe mental illness and requires compassion, it is inappropriate to tolerate abusive behavior. Be on the lookout for any form of abuse or maltreatment, whether physical, mental, emotional, verbal, sexual, or financial, and seek help immediately.

If you are in a non-abusive relationship with a narcissist, you must still establish clear boundaries and prioritize your own needs. Consider seeking treatment and the support of others in a similar situation. By strengthening your resilience and sense of self-worth, you will be better equipped to assist your spouse with NPD.

Implications Of Living With A Narcissist

You Lose Your Outside Relationships

When you are married to a narcissist, he will not want you to have relationships. He will attempt to gradually separate you from your peers and family. It may take some time to observe, as he will not explicitly state this as his goal.

It may begin with him making subtle remarks about his dislike for your friends. He may continuously want to spend time with you when you're supposed to be out with your friends, so you may choose to stay with him instead.

Be Wary Of Excuses

It is possible that he is ill when you are scheduled to visit your parents for the holidays, so he begs you to stay home with him. It is possible that he points out all the flaws or things that he finds bothersome about the people in your support network in order to convince you to share his viewpoint.

Spending additional time with your spouse...

His sense of entitlement towards your time will intensify. You begin to spend more time with him and rely on him to fulfill your needs. The more often this occurs, the less time you spend with others, until it appears that you have severed all ties with them.

And Spending Less Time With Friends

Although you may feel completely accepted by your partner, it may be difficult to perceive the reality of an emotionally abusive relationship. And without the aid of your external connections, it will become more difficult. Regardless of how loved you may feel by a partner with narcissistic personality disorder, it is essential to understand that this is not a healthy illustration of boundaries or "ideal love."

Low Self-Esteem

A narcissistic spouse will chip away at your sense of self-worth. A narcissist cannot tolerate when others are more successful than they are. They cannot tolerate admitting when they are wrong. This implies that you will never be the correct partner within the relationship. You will be mocked and degraded. This constant criticism will eventually damage your self-esteem.

residing with somebody, miss

You will begin to feel "not good enough" and "less than" your partner. Because he is privately insecure, his objective is to make himself feel better by making it appear as though he is superior to you. No one could ever match his ambitions or himself.

A Sense Of Entitlement

People with NPD may also thrive on the belief that they are the best you will ever get and that you should not abandon them. Their sense of entitlement towards the relationship will make you feel as though it would be foolish to leave. They could even threaten to depart in order to observe you pleading for them to stay. All of this stems from the low self-esteem they have instilled in you.

Feeling Like You're Going Crazy

Some narcissists engage in the practice known as gaslighting. It is a form of emotional torture that can leave you feeling as though you are going insane. Gaslighting is described as a form of persistent manipulation and indoctrination that leads the victim to doubt his or her perceptions, identity, and self-worth.

If this is the case, your husband incessantly lies and criticizes you. If you try to discuss it with him or call him out on his lies, he will deny it and become combative. Instead of accepting responsibility, he makes it appear as though you have the problem.

Repetitive Conduct

Even though you initially recognized that the problem was his, you eventually begin to embrace what he is saying and believe that the problem may be with you.

You May Question Yourself

As this continues, you begin to worry that you're losing your mind because you can't recall things he claims to have told you, or because he acts as if you didn't tell him something you know you did.

feeling lonely

Since he has pushed away your family and friends and isolated you, it appears that there is no one to whom you can turn to inquire about this. Even if you had someone to consult, you would likely be too terrified to speak for fear that they would also believe you to be insane.

Over time, such emotional mistreatment may be difficult to eradicate. However, there is a light at the end of the tunnel, so all is well. Before you can even begin to comprehend what an abusive relationship entails, you must learn to rely on yourself and your intuition. You're not delusional.

Constantly Needing to Concentrate on Making Him Happy

If your partner is a narcissist, your existence will likely revolve around making him happy. You will learn what to say and do to boost his ego because you cannot tolerate his behavior when you do not. He could become depressed, furious, impatient, or verbally aggressive. After repeatedly observing this behavior, you learn how to give him what he desires. Alternately, he may give you the cold shoulder or threaten to depart due to "unhappiness." This may not fit your conception of domestic abuse, but it is a narcissistic personality disorder-related abusive relationship trait.

narcissistic couple

When living with a narcissist, your existence revolves entirely around them. Over time, you begin to lose your identity. The extent to which your spouse governs your life will eventually cause you to abandon the plans and goals you had for your own life. You will observe that your friends are absent. You spend no time with your family, and your existence revolves entirely around your spouse.

You always end an argument by apologizing.

As previously stated, narcissists cannot tolerate acknowledging they are wrong. This means that they will not repent even if you and they are aware that they were in the wrong. Their sense of self-importance will enable them to surmount any obstacle. Every disagreement between the two of you will end with you accepting responsibility for it. Everything is your responsibility. Even circumstances beyond your control. They may suggest that you are doing everything incorrectly, including mundane tasks such as grocery shopping and laundry, and tell you that the marriage would be "perfect" if only you would change.

When a narcissist treats you in a certain way, especially if it's someone with whom you're in a relationship, you may experience a range of emotions. Occasionally, you may believe that everything is your responsibility. This makes you feel like a terrible person, which is detrimental to your self-esteem. Sometimes, being incessantly blamed for everything can irritate you. You are frustrated and resentful because you are unable to persuade your spouse that the situation is not your responsibility.

www.ingramcontent.com/pod-product-compliance
Lightning Source LLC
Chambersburg PA
CBHW050413120526
44590CB00015B/1952